Reading STREET

Grade 4

Scott Fo

Ten
Sent

PEARSON

Scott
Foresman

Editorial Offices: Glenview, Illinois • Parsippany, New Jersey • New York, New York
Sales Offices: Needham, Massachusetts • Duluth, Georgia • Glenview, Illinois
Coppell, Texas • Sacramento, California • Mesa, Arizona

ISBN: 0-328-16904-8

6 7 8 9 10 V034 11 10 09 08 07

Contents

Unit 1:   This Land Is Your Land

Unit 2:   Work & Play

Unit 3:   Patterns in Nature

Unit 4: Puzzles and Mysteries

Unit 5: Adventures by Land, Air, and Water

Unit 6: Reaching for Goals

Why Are Sentences So Important?

The sentence is the basic means of written communication. In order to be literate and articulate, students need to master sentence power.

When students read, they get information from sentences. Sentences provide facts and details, opinions, clues about the sequence of events, and information to understand cause and effect relationships. Students cannot get such meaning from sounds or words alone. Readers use sentences to build meaning in context and to decide on a main idea. You can think of the steps to comprehension as an inverted triangle, illustrating that comprehension is built upon the understanding that sounds create words that are parts of sentences which make up a text.

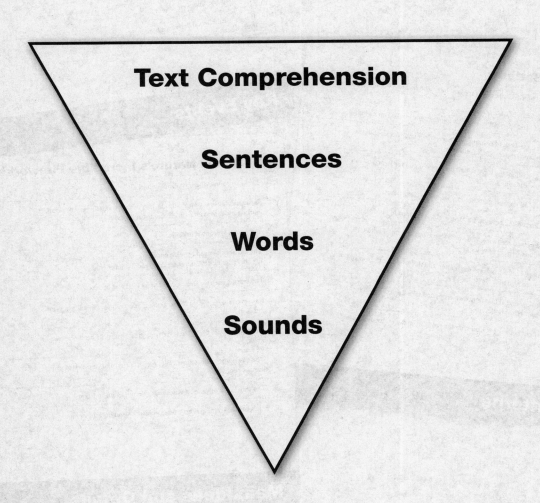

Text Comprehension

Sentences

Words

Sounds

In this booklet, Ten Important Sentences are provided for every selection in the Student Edition. Each sentence is logical and cohesive; each sentence provides a key idea from the selection. Together, the Ten Important Sentences help students make meaning in several ways. Depending on the genre, Ten Important Sentences can do any of the following:

- Present **key events** in a story or narrative nonfiction selection such as a biography or autobiography

- Give the stated **main ideas and details** in an essay or informational selection, or

- Demonstrate a predictable **pattern** in a selection, for example in a song, poem, or nonsense story

Gertrude Ederle

1. Gertrude Ederle was born on October 23, 1906.
2. She loved to swim.
3. By 1925 Trudy had set twenty-nine U.S. and world records.
4. She was determined to take on the ultimate challenge: the English Channel.
5. A newspaper editorial declared that Trudy wouldn't make it and that women must admit they would "remain forever the weaker sex."
6. She knew she would either swim the Channel or drown.
7. At about nine-forty at night, after more than fourteen hours in the water, Trudy's feet touched land.
8. She beat the men's record by almost two hours.
9. Reporters declared that the myth that women are the weaker sex was "shattered and shattered forever."
10. Gertrude Ederle had become a beacon of strength to girls and women everywhere.

Key Events

Tops & Bottoms

1. Once upon a time there lived a very lazy bear who had lots of money and lots of land.
2. So Hare and Mrs. Hare put their heads together and cooked up a plan.
3. "I'll do the hard work of planting and harvesting, and we can split the profit right down the middle," (said Hare).
4. Hare plucked off all the tops, tossed them into a pile for Bear, and put the bottoms aside for himself.
5. "But, Hare, all the best parts are in your half!" (said Bear).
6. Hare pulled off the bottoms for Bear and put the tops in his own pile.
7. "You've tricked me twice, and you owe me one season of both tops and bottoms!" (Bear growled).
8. Hare tugged off the roots at the bottom and the tassels at the top and put them in a pile for Bear.
9. "From now on I'll plant my own crops and take the tops, bottoms, and middles!" (Bear hollered).
10. Hare bought back his land with the profit from the crops, and he and Mrs. Hare opened a vegetable stand.

Patterns

Volcanoes: Nature's Incredible Fireworks

1. Every day somewhere volcanoes erupt.
2. If too much gas is trapped inside, part of the mountain may blow off, hurling rocks heavier than elephants for miles.
3. But not all volcanoes explode.
4. The answers lie deep beneath our feet in the four parts of the earth—the crust, the mantle, the outer core, and the inner core.
5. The crust, where we live, is covered by land and oceans.
6. It is several large pieces called plates that cover the planet like a giant jigsaw puzzle.
7. Where two plates meet, the force is so great that rocks bend or even break.
8. Where two plates meet, the mantle grows hotter, and volcanoes form near the edges.
9. Over thousands of years, a volcano may erupt again and again.
10. Scientists are learning what causes volcanoes and how they erupt.

Main Ideas and Details

How Ten Important Sentences Build Comprehension

Using and reusing *Ten Important Sentences* helps students build the skills they need for comprehension. *Ten Important Sentences* provides practical, selection-based instruction in these important skills:

• Recalling facts and details

• Finding and distinguishing between facts and opinions

• Arranging events in sequence

• Recognizing cause and effect relationships

• Identifying main idea and supporting details

You can help your students build their sentence power. Try these activities for building sentence power using *Ten Important Sentences*. The examples shown are from Grade 3. Match activities with other selections as you see fit.

Activity 1: Locate Sentences

1. Read the selection aloud to students or have students read all or parts of the selection silently.

2. Have students locate each of the Ten Important Sentences. (These will be those that tell the story or present the important ideas and details of the selection. The sentences on each master are in the correct order.) Discuss whether students agree with the choice of sentences. Which could they add or delete?

Activity 2: Distinguish Facts and Opinions

1. Read the selection aloud to students or have the students read all or parts of the selection silently. Discuss the selection, emphasizing sentences that are facts and sentences that are opinions.

2. Have students mark each of the Ten Important Sentences "F" for fact (something that can be proven) or "O" for opinion (something that a person believes or feels).

Me and Uncle Romie

1. Daddy thought it was a good time for me (James) to visit Uncle Romie and his wife, Aunt Nanette, up north in New York City.   **F**

2. No, I wasn't sure about this visit at all.   **O**

3. Home was like nothing I'd ever seen before.   **O**

4. "Your uncle's working very hard, so we won't see much of him for a while" (said Aunt Nanette).   **F**

5. My birthday was ruined.   **O**

6. Looking at Uncle Romie's paintings, I could feel Harlem—its beat and bounce.   **O**

7. "But the things we care about are pretty much the same" (said Uncle Romie).   **O**

8. Uncle Romie held up two tickets to a baseball game!   **F**

9. All these strangers talking to each other about their families and friends and special times, and all because of how my Uncle Romie's painting reminded them of things.   **F**

10. And then I was off on a treasure hunt, collecting things that reminded me of Uncle Romie.   **F**

Activity 3: Sequence Events

1. Read the selection aloud to students or have students read all or parts of the selection silently. Discuss the sequence of events, thoughts, or ideas in the selection.

2. Have students cut apart the Ten Important Sentences and mix the sentences in random order. Then have students order them correctly. (Note: Students can work with the sentences numbered or not, as you wish.)

Sequence
We all got together to build a church and a school.
Now this was a real boom town!

Activity 4: Link Cause and Effect

1. Read the selection aloud to students or have students read all or parts of the selection silently. Talk about events in the story and what causes them to happen.

2. Have students look at the Ten Important Sentences and find one or more pairs of sentences in which one sentence tells what happens and the other tells why it happens.

Cause
"There is more snow here than at home in England," said William.

Effect
He built a new roof with a very steep pitch and replaced the shingles.

Activity 5: Determine Main Idea

1. After reading, focus on the selection and talk with students about the big ideas.

2. Have students locate the sentences that provide the five elements of the main idea: who? did what? where? when? and why? Help students as they write the answers to these important questions in one sentence of their own.

Every day somewhere volcanoes erupt.

Notice that over time, students listen, manipulate sentences, and draw conclusions as they work toward comprehending what they have read. Using the Ten Important Sentences frees you from creating worksheets and lets you concentrate on helping students read and write with confidence.

The Main Idea Glove

U se the main idea glove to talk about the five elements of main idea. Duplicate this outline for each child or post it in your classroom. Your student will have the main idea right at hand!

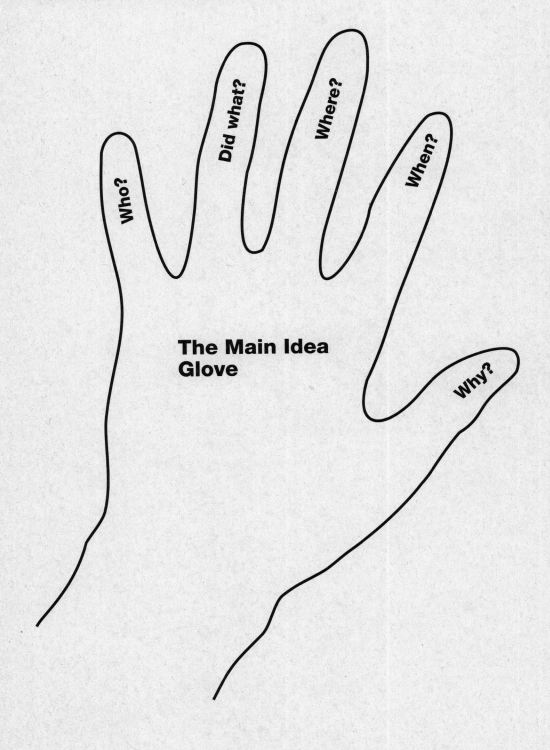

Who?

Did what?

Where?

When?

Why?

The Main Idea Glove

Because of Winn-Dixie

1. It all started with Winn-Dixie not liking it when I went into the library, because he couldn't go inside, too.

2. But I showed him how he could stand up on his hind legs and look in the window and see me in there, selecting my books; and he was okay, as long as he could see me.

3. This is what happened: I was picking out my books and kind of humming to myself, and all of a sudden, there was this loud and scary scream.

4. Once she was standing on her feet, she started acting all embarrassed, saying how I must think she was a silly old lady, mistaking a dog for a bear, but that she had a bad experience with a bear coming into the Herman W. Block Memorial Library a long time ago, and she never had quite gotten over it.

5. And before she could say yes or no, I went outside and got Winn-Dixie, and he came in and lay down with a "huummmppff" and a sigh, right at Miss Franny's feet.

6. So I (Miss Fanny) told him, I said, 'Daddy, I would most certainly love to have a library for my birthday, a small little library would be wonderful.'"

7. Well, one hot Thursday, I (Miss Fanny) was sitting in my library with all the doors and windows open and my nose stuck in a book, when a shadow crossed the desk.

8. "And standing right in front of me was a bear," (said Miss Fanny).

9. "I mean you and me and Winn-Dixie, we could all be friends," (said Opal).

10. I had just made my first friend in Naomi, and nobody was going to mess that up for me, not even old pinch-faced Amanda Wilkinson.

Lewis and Clark and Me

1. My life on the wharves was good, but I was a young dog and yearned for more.

2. Lewis wanted me.

3. I (Seaman) would follow this man (Lewis) to the ends of the Earth.

4. I have always loved the water, so the day we boarded the boat and pushed out onto the Ohio River was just about the happiest day of my life.

5. I could not believe my eyes; hundreds of squirrels were crossing the river.

6. I was going to get every squirrel in that river for Lewis.

7. All I know is that when I finished, there was a pile of squirrels in the boat.

8. As he talked on, it became obvious to me that the Indians were not interested in Lewis or what he was saying.

9. If that scrawny dog was the only dog they had seen, then I was a strange sight indeed.

10. All I can tell you is that when a dog and a man fit like Lewis and I did, nothing can separate them.

Grandfather's Journey

1. My grandfather was a young man when he left his home in Japan and went to see the world.

2. He explored North America by train and riverboat, and often walked for days on end.

3. The endless farm fields reminded him of the ocean he had crossed.

4. He shook hands with black men and white men, with yellow men and red men.

5. Of all the places he visited, he liked California best.

6. After a time, he returned to his village in Japan to marry his childhood sweetheart.

7. When I was a small boy, my favorite weekend was a visit to my grandfather's house.

8. When the war ended, there was nothing left of the city and of the house where my grandparents had lived.

9. The last time I saw him, my grandfather said that he longed to see California one more time.

10. The funny thing is, the moment I am in one country, I am homesick for the other.

The Horned Toad Prince

1. Reba Jo loved to twang her guitar and sing while the prairie wind whistled through the thirsty sagebrush.

2. As Reba Jo's lasso whirled into the air, a great gust of wind came whipping through the *arroyo* and blew her new cowgirl hat right off her head and down to the bottom of the dusty old well.

3. The horned toad looked at her slyly and said, "I'll fetch your *sombrero* for you if you will do *tres pequeños* favors for me."

4. "All you have to do is feed me some chili, play your *guitarra* for me, and let me take a *siesta* in your *sombrero,*" (said the horned toad).

5. Reba Jo placed the little critter in a splintered wooden bucket and carefully lowered him down the dry well, where he retrieved Reba Jo's hat.

6. "Now Reba Jo," said her daddy, "if you strike a bargain in these parts, a deal's a deal."

7. "Before I take my *siesta,* I have just one more favor to ask," said the horned toad.

8. "I can't believe I'm even considerin' this," she (Reba Jo) said, "but if it means you'll leave right now. . . pucker up, Lizard Lips."

9. When the dust cleared, there before Reba Jo stood a handsome young *caballero.*

10. "Now I'll be leaving as I promised," said Prince Maximillian José Diego López de España.

Letters Home from Yosemite

1. It (Yosemite) has incredible waterfalls, rock formations, alpine lakes and meadows, and giant sequoia trees.

2. It's located in the east central part of California and covers 1,170 square miles.

3. Yosemite was finally established as a national park on Oct. 1, 1890 by an act of Congress.

4. He (John Muir) fought hard to convince the U.S. government to preserve Yosemite as a national park.

5. Yosemite is right in the middle of the Sierra Nevada Mountains.

6. Native Americans were the first people to live in Yosemite, about 7,000 to 10,000 years ago.

7. Today, more than 3.5 million people visit the park every year.

8. More than half of America's highest waterfalls are found in Yosemite.

9. A sequoia tree can grow to over 300 feet tall and 40 feet around, and can live more than 3,000 years!

10. The park is also home to mountain lions, bobcats, coyotes, black-tailed jackrabbits, yellow-bellied marmots, rattlesnakes, and California bighorn sheep.

What Jo Did

1. Little Joanna Marie loved to play basketball.

2. Joanna saw rims on TV and figured they looked about the same height as her own—she had no idea they were only ten feet high.

3. As Joanna approached the other boys, she remembered that she had her hat on.

4. They probably think I'm a boy, she thought.

5. Finally, he (T.J.) was wide open for a jump shot when Jo came out of nowhere, jumped high into the air, and swatted his shot into the next court.

6. Her teammates encouraged her to shoot more, and when she did, they were amazed how the ball arced in the air like a rainbow before falling straight through the hoop, without touching the rim.

7. "I wanna see Joe dunk," (said the freckled-faced kid).

8. As the boys stared at her, Jo looked down at the ground and saw her hat lying there.

9. "Hey, she may be a girl, but I'd play on her team anytime," (said the kid with the Bulls jersey).

10. "You should come play with us again sometime," (said T.J.).

Coyote School News

1. My name is Ramón Ernesto Ramírez, but everybody calls me Monchi.

2. The real name of our ranch is Rancho San Isidro, after the patron saint of my great-grandfather, but most of the time everybody calls it the Ramírez Ranch.

3. We are a family of *vaqueros*.

4. Those are the most exciting days (roundup) of the year, even more exciting than Christmas.

5. I like Rosie, but I hate it when Natalia teases me.

6. All of us like Miss Byers, even the big kids, because she is young and nice and fair.

7. All week we have been working on our first *Coyote News*.

8. Everyday I am asking my father when we will have roundup.

9. When my father came over to Junior and me I thought he was going to tell us to go in to bed, but instead he said, " Tomorrow I want you boys to help with the branding."

10. "The winner of the *Coyote News* Writing Award is Ramón Ernesto Ramírez," (said Miss Byers).

Grace and the Time Machine

---

1. **AVA** And what have you got lined up for today?

---

2. **NANA** She's (Grace) been real helpful since I tripped over that silly cat and broke my ankle.

---

3. **RAJ** Well, all we have to do is to think of something that no one else has thought of.

---

4. **MARIA** Yeah, I think a time machine would be the best invention of all.

---

5. **RAJ** Well, the future's kind of scary.

---

6. **RAJ** What about the past?

---

7. **MARIA** Let's give Nana a turn!

---

8. **NANA** It's a wonderful machine that can take you back to when you were small.

---

9. **NANA** But you children seem to be bringing her (Mrs. Meyerson) back to life.

---

10. **AVA** What a wonderful invention!

Marven of the Great North Woods

1. As they entered the camp, the longest shadows Marven had ever seen stretched across the snow, and he realized with a start that the shadows were the lumberjacks walking in the moonlight.

2. "Starting tomorrow, you go into the bunkhouse and wake *les en retards*," (said Mr. Murray).

3. Marven took a deep breath, walked bravely over to the bed, reached out, and tapped the jack's shoulder.

4. "I'm no good as a bookkeeper and have enough other things to do around here," (said Mr. Murray).

5. By the end of the morning, Marven had a system and knew the name or symbol for each man.

6. Everyday the routine was simply meals and work, and Marven kept to his office and away from the lumberjacks as much as he could.

7. Here in the great north woods all was still and white.

8. He belonged in Duluth with them (his family), not in the middle of the great north woods with a grizzly.

9. "You think I was a grizzly!" (Jean Louis laughed).

10. Evening shadows fell through the trees, and as Marven skied alongside the huge men, he hummed the tune they were singing.

Name _____

So You Want to Be President?

1. There are good things about being President, and there are bad things about being President.

2. Lots of people want to be President.

3. Presidents have come in all shapes and sizes.

4. Though the Constitution says you'll have to wait until you're thirty-five, young, old, and in between have become President.

5. All kinds of pets have lived in the White House, mostly dogs.

6. Though most Presidents went to college, nine didn't: George Washington, Andrew Jackson, Martin Van Buren, Zachary Taylor, Millard Fillmore, Abraham Lincoln, Andrew Johnson, Grover Cleveland, and Harry Truman.

7. Almost any job can lead to the White House.

8. It (being President) can be wanting to turn lives around like Franklin Roosevelt, who provided soup and bread for the hungry, jobs for the jobless, and funds for the elderly to live on.

9. Every single Presidents has taken this oath: " I do solemnly swear (or affirm) that I will faithfully execute the office of President of the United States, and will to the best of my ability, preserve, protect and defend the Constitution of the United States."

10. Most of all, their past President first priority has always been the people and the country they served.

Name _____

The Stranger

----

1. It was the time of year Farmer Bailey liked best, when summer turned to fall.

----

2. But it wasn't a deer the farmer found lying in the road, it was a man.

----

3. She (Katy) heard her father whisper ". . . must be some kind of hermit. . . sort of fellow who lives alone in the woods."

----

4. "In a few days," the doctor said, "he should remember who he is and where he's from."

----

5. Instead of running into the woods, the rabbits took a hop in his direction.

----

6. The stranger could not take his eyes off the birds.

----

7. Farmer Bailey could not help noticing how peculiar the weather had been.

----

8. He (the stranger) held it (a leaf) in a trembling hand and, without thinking, blew on it with all his might.

----

9. By the tears in his eyes the Baileys could tell that their friend had decided to leave.

----

10. And etched in frost on the farmhouse windows are words that say simply, "See you next fall."

Adelina's Whales

1. La Laguna is the name of a quiet, dusty fishing village on the sandy shore of Laguna San Ignacio, in Baja California, Mexico.

2. In late January, every afternoon after school, Adelina walks to the beach to see if her friends—the gray whales—have returned.

3. The scientists who have come to visit and study the whales have explained that Laguna San Ignacio is the perfect place for the mother whales to have their babies and then teach them how to swim.

4. This is the only place on earth where these giant gray whales—totally wild animals—choose to seek out the touch of a human hand.

5. The whales have been coming to this lagoon for hundreds of years, and Adelina is proud that her grandfather, Pachico, was the first person to tell of a "friendly" visit with one.

6. With brains as large as a car's engine, gray whales might even have their own language.

7. Although her home is a simple shack on a sandy bluff hugging the edge of the Pacific Ocean, Adelina has many new friends who come to share her world.

8. Sometimes she giggles with delight at the idea of being the first girl to captain a panga (a small open fishing boat) and teach people about the whales in the lagoon.

9. This is the place where two worlds join together.

10. Maybe, as the whales sleep, they dream of the colorful sunsets of Laguna San Ignacio.

How Night Came

1. Long, long ago, at the very beginning of time, when the world had just been made, there was no night.

2. With sorrow and with longing, the daughter left her home in the deep ocean and came to live with her husband in the land of daylight.

3. "Oh, how I wish night would come," she (Iemanjá's daughter) cried.

4. "You must beg her to give you some of the darkness of night so that my wife will stop longing to return to her mother's kingdom and will be able to find happiness on land with me," (said the husband).

5. "But," she (Iemanjá) said, " you must not open this until you reach my daughter, because only she can calm the night spirits I have packed inside."

6. "I am going to open the bag and see what makes all those terrible sounds," (said the third servant).

7. And when she (Iemanjá's daughter) spoke, the night spirits were suddenly calmed, and there was hushed darkness everywhere.

8. To Iemanjá's daughter, this coming of night was indeed like the quiet after crying or the end of the storm.

9. To the last bright star still shining above the palm tree she (Iemanjá's daughter) said, "Glittering star, from now on you will be our sign that night is passing."

10. To this day, the gifts of Iemanjá's daughter help celebrate each new sunrise.

Ten Important Sentences • *Unit 3, Week 3*

Eye of the Storm

1. Storms are caused by certain kinds of weather patterns.

2. Because Warren is a storm chaser, his life also follows these weather patterns.

3. "When a hurricane is forming, I look at satellite pictures, I listen to weather forecasters talk about it, and I pay attention to what scientists and meteorologists think the hurricane is going to do," (said Warren).

4. "Hurricanes are the only type of storm where I'm shooting destruction in progress," (said Warren).

5. "Finding a place to stay safe while I take hurricane photos is also a challenge," (said Warren).

6. Hurricane Andrew was expected to hit the Florida coast in two days, so Mike, Steve, and Warren had agreed to work together to predict where the storm was going to hit, scout out a safe place to stay, and photograph the storm.

7. The winds were carrying raindrops sideways through the air.

8. Now the winds were blowing so hard inside the garage that it was impossible to walk even a few feet in areas that weren't blocked by walls.

9. Warren took pictures of the wind bending the trees near the marina and the broken boats on the shore.

10. Still, as the airplane took off from Miami, it was hard for Warren to imagine that two nights earlier he had been watching, listening to, and photographing the destructive winds of Hurricane Andrew.

The Great Kapok Tree

1. Now all was quiet as the creatures watched the two men and wondered why they had come.

2. The larger man stopped and pointed to a great Kapok tree.

3. Before he (the smaller man) knew it, the heat and hum of the forest had lulled him to sleep.

4. A bee buzzed in the sleeping man's ear: "Senhor, my hive is in this Kapok tree, and I fly from tree to tree and flower to flower collecting pollen."

5. "Senhor!" squawked the toucan, "you must not cut down this tree."

6. "You will leave many of us homeless if you chop down this great Kapok tree," (piped the tree frog).

7. He (the jaguar) growled in his ear: "Senhor, the Kapok tree is home to many birds and animals."

8. "If you destroy the beauty of the rain forest, on what would you feast your eyes?" (asked the three-toed sloth).

9. Before him stood the rain forest child, and all around him, staring, were the creatures who depended upon the great Kapok tree.

10. Then he dropped the ax and walked out of the rain forest.

The Houdini Box

1. Children liked Houdini because he could do the unexplainable things that they wanted to do.

2. Victor's mother was going crazy unlocking her son from trunks, reminding him to breathe when he took a bath, and telling him not to walk into walls.

3. Victor was looking around the huge, bustling train station when he saw, way across the crowds, Harry Houdini himself, buying tickets with his wife.

4. "I'll write you (Victor) a letter," (said Houdini).

5. Victor thought and dreamt about the magician's letter.

6. She (Mrs. Houdini) came to Victor and handed him a small locked box.

7. Then she (Mrs. Houdini) opened the front door, and as she showed him out, he heard her whisper, "Houdini died today."

8. This wasn't Houdini's box at all!

9. Before he became Houdini, the magician had been a boy named Ehrich Weiss.

10. And that night, while his wife and son slept downstairs and the attic shadows vanished in the pale, blue fall of moonlight, Victor locked himself inside his grandmother's trunk and escaped in under twenty seconds.

Encantado: Pink Dolphin of the Amazon

1. Everything about them sounds impossible: pink dolphins!

2. They don't look like "regular" dolphins, either: Unlike the ones who swim in the sea, the pink dolphin doesn't have a tall, pointed fin on the back, sticking out of the water like a shark's.

3. Besides making sounds from their mouths, dolphins (as well as many whales) can also send out pulses of sound, like an invisible beam of light, from inside their foreheads.

4. In fact, the echoes form a three-dimensional image in the dolphin's brain, allowing the animal to "see" not only the object's shape and size but also its insides.

5. Pink dolphins can bend their bodies to twist gracefully through the underwater treetops.

6. Canoeing through the flooded forest feels like a dream.

7. Today he's (Moises) taking you to this favorite lake, where he knows you'll see pink dolphins.

8. You twirl around, but all you see is the dolphin's wake, the wave it made when it dived just a split second ago.

9. Most animals, including dolphins, look as different from one another as people do.

10. "The bufeo, they are very mysterious," he (Moises) says.

The King in the Kitchen

1. **PEASANT** The princess thinks I'm wonderful, and I think she's wonderful.

2. **COOK** Oh, dear, the King didn't like the soup and I took such trouble with it.

3. **KING** I could make a better soup than that with my eyes shut.

4. **KING** Whoever can guess what this is, wins a reward.

5. **KING** Now, Duke, can you tell me what I've made here in this bowl?

6. **PRINCESS** He doesn't know what you've made so I don't have to marry him.

7. **PEASANT** You have just made a bowl of the most wonderful glue I've ever seen.

8. **PEASANT** We'll put this in bottles and sell it everywhere.

9. **KING** What will my Prime Minister say when he hears I am to have a peasant for a son-in-law?

10. **PEASANT** When we tell him (the Prime Minister) how much money will go into the Royal Treasury from your glue, he won't care about anything.

Name _____

Seeker of Knowledge

1. In 1790, a French boy named Jean-François Champollion was born.

2. "Then I will one day," said Jean-François, and he left the house full of enthusiasm, sure that he would be the first to discover the key to Egyptian hieroglyphs.

3. He (Jean François) could not read the Egyptian words, but he dreamed that one day he would, as he sailed up the Nile.

4. When Jean-François finished school at sixteen, his brother took him to Paris to meet the scholars who were studying a black stone from Rosetta, Egypt.

5. Once, even Napoleon came to Grenoble and sat up all night, listening spellbound as Jean-François told the great man of his dreams.

6. When Jean-François was thirty, he gathered up his notebooks and left Grenoble.

7. In Paris, Jean-François studied the Rosetta Stone and other inscriptions.

8. Jean-François studied the names and saw the link!

9. People all over France celebrated his triumph as Jean-François became the first to translate the ancient writing and open the door to Egypt's past.

10. As Jean-François had imagined a thousand times in his dreams, he sailed up the Nile.

Encyclopedia Brown

1. But there was something out of the ordinary about Idaville: For more than a year, no child or grown-up had gotten away with breaking a law.

2. No, the brains behind it all was his ten-year-old son, Encyclopedia.

3. "There was a theft at the aquarium today," he (Chief Brown) said, rubbing his forehead.

4. Encyclopedia put down his fork and listened carefully as his father explained that Fred, a tiger salamander, had been stolen.

5. "Employees and volunteers are the only ones who have access to the back room in the Den of Darkness where Fred was being kept," (said Chief Brown).

6. Chief Brown told Encyclopedia and Mrs. Brown that three people had been working at the exhibit that morning: Mrs. King, who volunteered at the aquarium every Monday; Sam Maine, the man in charge of cleaning and maintaining the exhibits; and Dr. O'Donnell, an expert on reptiles and amphibians.

7. They knew that when Encyclopedia closed his eyes, it meant he was doing his deepest thinking.

8. "Sam told me he's been taking care of salamanders and other lizards for more than nineteen years," (said Chief Brown).

9. "Sam Maine is lying, and I can prove it!" (declared Encyclopedia).

10. Anyone who'd been taking care of salamanders for that long would know that salamanders are not lizards.

Sailing Home

1. My sister Dagmar, my brother, Albert, and I, Matilda, grew up aboard the *John Ena*, a four-masted sailing bark that carried cargo all over the world.

2. The *John Ena* had bedrooms, a bathroom, and a main saloon that was a combination living room with a pink marble fireplace and a dining room with a big round table.

3. We all took turns caring for our pets as we traveled around the world.

4. Instead of a backyard or a playground we had a great wooden deck where we played tag, hide-and-seek, and catch, always with beanbags, because balls bounced overboard.

5. There were no radios then, and when we were out at sea we seldom saw another ship.

6. With Miss Shipman in charge, we went to school at the dining table six days a week, mornings and afternoons, with only an hour off for lunch and no recesses.

7. The crew watched us all the time to make sure we didn't get into serious trouble.

8. Even though our life was different from other children's, we didn't miss out on anything.

9. That year, as we crossed the China Sea, the weather turned wild.

10. We were at home, home on the sea.

Lost City

1. Sixty miles south, in Cusco, Hiram Bingham gazed thoughtfully at the old Incan stone wall.

2. But right here was the most beautiful stonework he had ever seen— huge stones cut so perfectly that not even a razor blade could be slipped between them.

3. The Inca had no iron tools to carve them, no wheel or draft animals to move them.

4. Bingham's determination to find the lost city grew with each turn of the increasingly wild trail.

5. "Are there any ruins nearby?" Bingham asked when Arteaga ventured into camp.

6. "There are very good ruins on top of the mountain called Machu Picchu," (through the interpreter, the farmer said).

7. Sergeant Carrasco thought about his good sturdy shoes; Bingham thought of nothing but the lost city.

8. The boy's whole family crowded around to greet the exhausted travelers, then brought gourds of cool water and boiled sweet potatoes.

9. He (Bingham) began to see the outlines of a city!

10. He had stumbled on Machu Picchu, a city lost in time, a city lost in the clouds.

Amelia and Eleanor Go for a Ride

1. Amelia and Eleanor were birds of a feather.

2. But Eleanor was Eleanor Roosevelt, the First Lady of the United States, who lived in the White House with her husband, President Franklin Roosevelt.

3. Amelia was Amelia Earhart, the celebrated aviator who had been the first female pilot to fly solo across the Atlantic Ocean.

4. Besides, she (Eleanor) loved the feeling of independence she had when she was behind the wheel.

5. Dinner started with George Washington's crab chowder.

6. "Mrs. Roosevelt just received her student pilot's license," said one of the reporters.

7. Very few people in the whole world had ever flown at night, and Amelia was one of them.

8. "How amusing it is to see a girl in a white evening dress and high-heeled shoes flying a plane!" Eleanor said.

9. As the Secret Service agents drove them slowly back to the White House, Amelia and Eleanor agreed that there was nothing quite as exciting as flying.

10. With the wind in their hair and the brisk air stinging their cheeks, they flew down the road.

Antarctic Journal

1. Depart from home in the early morning, to be gone four months to Antarctica, a part of the planet as remote as the moon in its own way.

2. For millions of years Antarctica, the fifth largest continent, has been in the grip of an ice age.

3. There is too much to take in—rolling seas, salt spray, broad-winged seabirds soaring inches above the wave tops.

4. The sun never sets.

5. It's good to know an ocean exists where whales have the right of way over ships.

6. Litchfield is three miles from Palmer by zodiac, a protected island visited by two or three people a year.

7. Each island has an emergency cache of food and supplies, marked with a flag, available if a person gets stranded during a storm.

8. I have learned that the largest animal on Earth, the hundred-ton blue whale, eats only one of the smallest animals on Earth: krill (*Euphausia supurba*).

9. A crack had appeared under me, a crevasse in the glacier.

10. The egg reminds me of my trip to the place where penguins raise downy chicks, krill swarm in numbers greater than stars in the sky, whales have rights, and icebergs drift in graceful arcs across Southern Ocean swells.

Moonwalk

1. Gerry Kandel hated it when his older brother (Vern) called him Runt.

2. Dad had left them at the shelter and gone off with the tractor to inspect the new telescope that was being built still farther out on the crater floor.

3. Now he (Gerry) was jumping over gullies in the bare, dark ground.

4. He (Gerry) took four running steps, then soared over the rille.

5. "Dad told us to stay inside the shelter," said Gerry.

6. Turning to look back across the rille at Vern, he (Gerry) called, "Nothing to it!"

7. Gerry rushed to the edge of the gully and saw his brother halfway down the rille, lying motionless.

8. As long as we stay in the night we'll be OK, Gerry told himself.

9. Blinking sweat from his eyes, trying hard not to cry, grunting, puffing hard, Gerry dragged Vern to the shelter.

10. "You saved my life!" (said Vern to Gerry).

My Brother Martin

1. They called me Christine, and like three peas in one pod, we grew together.

2. And although Daddy, who was an important minister, and Mother Dear, who was known far and wide as a musician, often had work that took them away from home, our grandmother was always there to take care of us.

3. "Why do white people treat colored people so mean?" M.L. asked Mother Dear afterward.

4. And with me and M.L. and A.D. standing in front of her trying our best to understand, Mother Dear gave the reason behind it all.

5. He (M.L) said, "Mother Dear, one day I'm going to turn this world upside down."

6. Back in a time when certain places in our country had unfair laws that said it was right to keep black people separate because our skin was darker and our ancestors had been captured in far-off Africa and brought to America as slaves.

7. The thought of *not* playing with those kids because they were different, because they were white and we were black, never entered our minds

8. He (Daddy) always stood up for himself when confronted with hatred and bigotry, and each day he shared his encounters at the dinner table.

9. But my brother never forgot the example of our father, or the promise he had made to our mother on the day his friends turned him away.

10. And when he was much older, my brother M.L. dreamed a dream. . . that turned the world upside down.

Ten Important Sentences • *Unit 6, Week 1*

Jim Thorpe's Bright Path

1. They say Jim Thorpe's story began in May of 1887 in a small log cabin on the North Canadian River.

2. He (Jim) was so fast and had so much endurance that he could run down a rabbit on foot.

3. The Indian Agency that oversaw the reservation said that when Sac and Fox children reached age six, they had to go to the Agency Boarding School.

4. "My sons," he said to Jim and Charlie, "you need white man's knowledge to survive."

5. It was no surprise that Jim hated school.

6. He would never hear Charlie's encouraging voice again.

7. Carlisle was always looking for Indian students who were good athletes, and the recruiter had heard of Jim's success as a runner at Haskell.

8. "I want you to show other races what an Indian can do," (said Pa Thorpe).

9. Before long Jim Thorpe was Carlisle's best track athlete.

10. His education had put his feet on the bright path.

Tía Lola

1. Miguel tries to imagine the grouchy old man at Rudy's Restaurant as the young boy with the friendly smile in the photograph.

2. Two days later, Colonel Charlebois's answer is in their mailbox.

3. "I would be honored to have the team practice in my back pasture," he (Colonel Charlebois) replies in a shaky hand as if he'd written the letter while riding in a car over a bumpy road.

4. As they slurp and lick, she (Tía Lola) practices her English by telling them wonderful stories about Dominican baseball players like Sammy Sosa and the Alou brothers and Juan Marichal and Pedro and Ramón Martínez.

5. The front porch is the color of a bright bruise.

6. "Colonel Charlebois is going to throw a fit," (said Mami).

7. "Unless the house is back to its original white by the end of the month, you are welcome to move out," (wrote Colonel Charlebois).

8. Which color will the whole house end up being?

9. Out file nine boys in purple-and-white striped uniforms and purple baseball caps..

10. He (Miguel) lifts his arm and throws the ball at the young boy - and the old man catches it.

Name _____

To Fly: The Story of the Wright Brothers

1. One of Orville's best money-making ideas was to build kites to sell to his friends.

2. And he (Orville) also made an important discovery that he would use later—curved wings fly better than flat ones.

3. They (Orville and Wilbur) both enjoyed fixing bicycles, too—so much so that they opened a bicycle shop in 1893 and moved the printing business upstairs.

4. Chanute was to become the Wright brothers' greatest supporter.

5. How could a person *control* his flight once he was in the air?

6. If they could make the wings of a two-winged glider flex like this, they could control its flight!

7. For the next three years the brothers built gliders of various shapes and tested them on the Atlantic seashore near the village of Kitty Hawk.

8. During the winter of 1902-03, Orville and Wilbur built a motor and propellers for their aircraft.

9. The Flyer had taken off from level ground, moved through the air under its own power, and landed on a place that was level with its takeoff point.

10. The Age of Aviation had begun.

Far Side of the Moon

1. It is July 20, 1969.

2. It is -250°F (-180°C) in the shade and +250°F (+120°C) in the sun at the Sea of Tranquility, where Neil and Buzz have landed the *Eagle*.

3. Neil Armstrong is the first man on the moon.

4. Neil and Buzz stay on the moon for 21 hours and 36 minutes, but only a little more than 2 hours of that time is spent outside the lunar module.

5. The moon has a smell.

6. Six hundred million people in 47 countries are watching the blurred TV transmission of the lunar landing.

7. When Neil and Buzz are on the moon's surface, Michael Collins has to do three people's jobs.

8. Ever since they left the moon, the astronauts have been eager to get back home.

9. To find out if the astronauts are carrying deadly germs, mice are let into the quarantine trailer.

10. When Michael Collins returned from the moon, he made a decision to never travel again